Squirrels

by **Steven Otfinoski**

mc **Marshall Cavendish** Benchmark

New York

Thanks to Larry Battson, Wildlife Educational Services, Inc., for his expert reading of this manuscript.

Copyright © 2011 Marshall Cavendish Corporation

Published by Marshall Cavendish Benchmark
An imprint of Marshall Cavendish Corporation

Other Marshall Cavendish Offices:
Marshall Cavendish International (Asia) Private Limited, 1 New Industrial Road, Singapore 536196 • Marshall Cavendish International (Thailand) Co Ltd. 253 Asoke, 12th Flr, Sukhumvit 21 Road, Klongtoey Nua, Wattana, Bangkok 10110, Thailand • Marshall Cavendish (Malaysia) Sdn Bhd, Times Subang, Lot 46, Subang Hi-Tech Industrial Park, Batu Tiga, 40000 Shah Alam, Selangor Darul Ehsan, Malaysia

Marshall Cavendish is a trademark of Times Publishing Limited

All websites were available and accurate when this book was sent to press.

Library of Congress Cataloging-in-Publication Data
Otfinoski, Steven.
Squirrels / by Steven Otfinoski.
p. cm. — (Animals animals)
Includes index.
Summary: "Provides comprehensive information on the anatomy, special skills, habitats, and diet of squirrels"—Provided by publisher.
ISBN 978-0-7614-4843-3
1. Squirrels—Juvenile literature. I. Title.
QL737.R68O84 2011
599.36—dc22
2009022628

Photo research by Joan Meisel

Cover photo: Frits Van Daalen/Minden Pictures

The photographs in this book are used by permission and through the courtesy of:
Alamy: Island Road Images, 8; Rick & Nora Bowers, 10; Juniors Bildarchiv, 12; T.M.O.Pets, 19; Paik Photography, 22; Paul Prince Photography, 30; Evan Bowen-Jones,34; John James, 38;; Robert Sadura, 39. *Animals Animals - Earth Scenes*: Krishnan, M., 9. *Corbis*: Wolfgang Kaehler, 7, 17. *Getty Images*: Tim Graham, 1; Georgette Douwma, 4; Frank Schneidermeyer, 14; Elliott Neep, 16; Paul McCormick, 20; Hope Ryden, 27; Mark Hamblin, 28; David Courtenay, 32. *Minden Pictures*: Sumio Harada, 24, 26. *Photo Researchers, Inc.*: Nicholas Bergkessel, 11; Steve Maslowski, 37.

Editor: Joy Bean
Publisher: Michelle Bisson
Art Director: Anahid Hamparian
Series Designer: Adam Mietlowski

Printed in Malaysia (T)
1 3 5 6 4 2

Contents

Squirrels, Squirrels, Everywhere

For most of us, few wild animals are as present in our daily lives as squirrels. In the spring, we watch them chase each other noisily across our backyards and up and down trees. In the fall, we see them scampering around, storing away nuts and acorns for the cold weather ahead. In the winter, some of us hear them scurrying around in our attics and walls, unwelcome guests in our homes. Yes, squirrels appear to be everywhere. There are at least 260 different *species*, or kinds, of squirrels, and they live on every *continent* except for Australia and Antarctica.

There is a lot about these furry little *mammals* that might surprise you. For example, did you know that

Most people in the United States can see at least one squirrel every day. Squirrels can usually be seen scurrying up trees or collecting food.

squirrels are actually members of the *rodent* family? Like mice, rats, guinea pigs, and other rodents, squirrels have large, sharp front teeth that are made for *gnawing* through the shells of nuts or enlarging a hole in a tree for a nest.

Most squirrels fall into two main categories— ground squirrels and tree squirrels. Ground squirrels include chipmunks, marmots, and prairie dogs. They have short tails and never climb trees. They usually make their homes in holes or burrows in the ground. Their burrows often have several separate rooms, or *chambers*. There may be a chamber for sleeping, one for storage, and another that the squirrel uses as a nursery for its young. Each burrow usually has two entrances. If one entrance is blocked by snow or a predator, the squirrel can escape through the other entrance.

Tree squirrels include gray squirrels, red squirrels, and flying squirrels. They have long, bushy tails and make their nests of twigs and leaves, called *dreys*, on tree branches or in the hollows of trees.

Did You Know . . .

The word *squirrel* comes from the Greek words *skia*, meaning "shadow", and *oura*, meaning "tail". From observation, the ancient Greeks believed the squirrel sat in the shade of its tail to avoid the hot sun.

This ground squirrel peeks out from its nest in the ground.

Species Chart

◆ The gray squirrel is a tree squirrel that is native to North America. It can also be found in Great Britain, Ireland, and South Africa. It is 16 to 20 inches (41 to 51 centimeters) long, including its tail. It weighs 1.5 pounds (0.68 kilograms). These squirrels may be called gray squirrels, but they come in other colors, including white, and black. The gray squirrel can leap more than 20 feet (6.1 meters) in the air.

A gray squirrel.

◆ The Indian giant squirrel is one of the largest species of squirrels. It grows to a length of 36 inches (91 cm) and weighs 4.4 pounds (2 kg). It is a tree squirrel and lives in southern Asia. The Indian giant squirrel rarely comes down to the ground and can jump from one tree to another up to a distance of 28 feet (9 m).

An Indian giant squirrel.

A 13-lined ground squirrel.

◆ The 13-lined ground squirrel lives in the central United States and Canada. It is 6 to 11 inches (15 to 28 cm) in length and weighs 4 to 9 ounces (113 to 255 g). Its body is marked with thirteen alternating brown and white lines, sometimes broken into spots, that give it its name. Like most ground squirrels, the 13-lined ground squirrel *hibernates* in the winter. It will go into its burrow in October and usually will not emerge again until March.

◆ The southern flying squirrel is one of the smallest of the tree squirrels and one of the few squirrels that are *nocturnal,* or active at night. It grows to a length of 10 inches (25 cm), including its tail. Flying squirrels do not actually fly but rather glide from tree branch to tree branch or tree to tree. They have loose flaps of skin connecting their front legs to their hind legs. These flaps act as parachutes when they leap off a branch. The flying squirrel can glide a distance of up to 150 feet (46 m).

A southern flying squirrel.

Red squirrels are easily identifiable by the tufts of red fur that grow from the ends of their ears.

Although squirrels come in many different shapes and sizes, they share certain common characteristics. Most of them have slender bodies covered by fur. Gray and red squirrels—both tree squirrels—have white fur on their underparts. Their upper bodies, however, can be a mixture of several colors despite their names. Gray squirrels can be gray, black, white, tan, or brown. Red squirrels can be red, gray, or tan. The tails of most tree squirrels are long and bushy, while ground squirrels have shorter tails. A tree squirrel uses its tail in a number of ways. It provides balance when the squirrel is climbing trees. If the squirrel should lose its balance and fall, its tail acts like a parachute and breaks its fall. When it rains, the tail serves as an umbrella, and at night when it is cold, the squirrel can wrap its tail around itself like a warm blanket.

Most squirrels have round ears and large, black eyes. Their vision is excellent, and they see in color. Their eyes are located on the sides of their head, allowing them to have a wide range of vision. Both their forepaws and hind paws have sharp claws that allow tree squirrels to scamper up and down trees with the greatest of ease. The claws also give ground squirrels a weapon to defend themselves against *predators*.

Searching, Eating, Storing

If you have ever seen a tree squirrel collecting and storing its food, you know how much time and energy this little animal spends on these activities. And for good reasons. Unlike ground squirrels, tree squirrels do not hibernate during the winter. Hibernating animals go into a deep sleep in winter during which their heart rate and body temperature drop drastically. In this deep sleep, they do not need to eat. Their bodies live off stored fat. But tree squirrels are active in winter and need to keep eating in order to stay alive. In the winter, they will dig up their stored food.

In the summer and fall, the squirrel makes a small hole in the ground with its forepaw. Then it drops a nut

An eastern gray squirrel brings a nut to its nest in a tree in Tennessee.

15

or acorn into the hole. Next, it covers up the hole with soil or dead leaves that it pats down with its paws and nose. At other times, the squirrel deposits food in a hollow tree. One squirrel may bury hundreds of these hidden treasures all over its *territory*, the area it lives and feeds in. How does it find the food later? It relies on its keen sense of smell and not its memory. Sometimes the squirrel will find food buried by another squirrel. And some of the food it buries never gets dug up again. Many of these buried acorns will grow into trees.

We think of squirrels eating nuts, seeds, and acorns. But that is only one part of their varied diet.

Squirrels will bury their food in various locations. This squirrel is burying its prize in the ground.

Squirrels also eat tree bark, mushrooms, berries, and all kinds of fruits and grains. Many squirrels are *omnivores* that eat animals as well as plants. They will eat caterpillars and other insects as well as young birds, frogs, lizards, and even rabbits.

Just as squirrels have many places they store food, so many of them have more than one home. Most tree squirrels have at least three nests in trees or on tree

This eastern fox squirrel looks out from its nest in a tree.

branches. Some have as many as ten homes. Why? Being close to one or more of their food sources is one reason. It also provides them with a ready escape route from a predator. A third reason is that if one home is invaded by a pest, such as fleas, the squirrel can move to another home.

Ground squirrels create their nests in holes or burrows in the earth or in stone walls, log piles, or the rotting stumps of trees. Flying squirrels will live in trees, but when the weather turns cold, they will invade sheds, barns, birdhouses, and even the attics of houses.

Wherever a squirrel lives, it will defend its territory fiercely. If another squirrel or other animal should enter its territory to hunt for food, the squirrel will raise a ruckus. Gray squirrels make a funny clicking sound when another squirrel has entered its territory. Red squirrels make a scratchy sound. Fox squirrels cluck and bark. Flying squirrels squeak. All these noises mean one thing—"Get out of my territory!" These vocal warnings are usually accompanied by strong body language—foot stomping and tail twitching. If the warning

Did You Know . . .
If it had to, a red squirrel could live as long as two years on the food it hides away in holes in the ground and in trees.

18

Squirrels enjoy eating a variety of different foods. This gray squirrel takes time to munch on some grapes.

When threatened by a predator, squirrels will make noises to warn its enemy to keep away.

does not scare off the invader, the squirrel will attack and even kill the unwelcome squirrel.

One of the few times that a squirrel may be happy to see another squirrel of the opposite sex is during mating season.

3 Moms and Their Pups

Squirrels are ready to mate when they are close to a year old. Most *breed* twice a year—in midwinter and in spring. The mating rite of squirrels is not a graceful dance but a wild chase. Males pursue females around and around on the ground and up and down trees. The female decides with whom she wants to mate. She will allow the mate she chooses to catch her.

After mating, the male squirrel leaves and plays no part in raising its young, called *pups*. They are born about thirty-six to forty-five days after the adults mate. Tree squirrels usually give birth to a *litter* of three to five pups, while ground squirrels can give birth to three to ten pups at a time.

A male fox tree squirrel (left) nuzzles a female squirrel (right), hoping she will mate with him.

23

The pups enter the world completely helpless. They have no fur or teeth, and their eyes and ears are sealed shut. They weigh only 0.5 ounces (14 g). Flying squirrels at birth weigh less than half that. Blind, the pups feel their way to their mother with short, stiff whiskers called *vibrissae*. Once they find her, they nestle up against her warm body and nurse on her milk through her *teats*.

When the pups are about three weeks old, they have a little fur on their backs and have grown two teeth. The eyes and ears of gray squirrels open at five

Newborn red squirrels lay helpless in their nest.

weeks, and they can see and hear. Red squirrels' and flying squirrels' eyes and ears open a week to ten days earlier. The mother squirrel will only leave her pups during this critical time to find food for herself. If a predator, such as a snake, should try to attack and eat her pups, she will defend them fiercely. California ground squirrel pups have a unique defense against the rattlesnake, one of their main predators. The pups find the *molted* skin of a rattlesnake and chew on it. The skin gives off a scent that covers the pups' own scent. Rattlers find prey largely through the sense of smell. A passing rattler does not smell the pups but rather the scent of another rattler and leaves the pups alone. By the eighth week, the pups no longer need their mother's milk but can live solely on solid foods. The mother takes them out for short trips. They learn how to find food and play with one another. Play is good exercise that makes them stronger. They march behind their mother along tree branches, learning from her example how to climb and jump from branch to branch.

By about three months, the pups are ready to leave the nest and find their own

Did You Know . . .
The female tree squirrel attracts a male by making a quacking sound like a duck.

A mother red squirrel lies with her babies to keep them safe and warm.

homes. By the following winter or spring, they will be ready to have their own litters. Most kinds of squirrels can live as long as ten to fifteen years. But few do. Most are killed after only four to five years by one of the many dangers that surround them.

Three young red squirrels leave their nest to explore their world.

Victims and Invaders

Squirrels have lots of enemies. Coyotes, bobcats, foxes, pine martens, wolves, raccoons, and snakes all eat squirrels in the wild. Eagles, hawks, and owls swoop down and devour them from the sky. In your backyard, squirrels are potential prey to your pet cat or dog.

The main defense weapons most squirrels have to fend off their attackers are their sharp front teeth and claws. Sometimes a flick of a tree squirrel's long, bushy tail will send a predator running. If attacked by a rattlesnake, a tree squirrel can use its tail in a unique way to save itself. It can actually raise the

Eagles are one of the greatest enemies of squirrels. They can swoop down from the sky and grab a squirrel off the ground.

temperature of its tail, which helps when rattlesnakes are after them. Rattlesnakes determine their prey by body heat. When the tail heats up, it may confuse the snake or make it think the squirrel is another, larger kind of animal. For whatever reason, the rattler

One way squirrels can defend themselves is by fighting with their long, sharp claws.

retreats. In most cases, however, the squirrel's best defense is flight. Tree squirrels can scamper up trees and ground squirrels can scurry down into their burrows to get away.

Squirrels are also threatened by diseases. Squirrel pox is a *virus* to which some squirrels, such as the gray squirrel, have built up an *immunity* over time. But other types of squirrels, such as the red squirrel, have no immunity to squirrel pox and can die within four or five days of being infected.

This disease has become a serious problem in Europe since the introduction of the gray squirrel in the late nineteenth and early twentieth centuries. Gray squirrels were brought to Great Britain from North America at that time because some people thought they would add to the beauty of many of England's stately homes. The gray squirrel had no predators in England and experienced a population explosion. The large number of gray squirrels drove the native red squirrel from its habitat and carried the squirrel pox virus that killed many red squirrels. Today the red squirrel is an endangered species, not only in England

Did You Know . . .
When a predator grabs a squirrel by its tail, the tail will break off, giving the squirrel a chance to escape.

The red squirrel population in England is low because of the invasion of the gray squirrel on its territory.

but in Ireland and Italy as well, due to the invasion of the gray squirrel. Authorities in these countries are seeking solutions to containing the gray squirrel population by hunting and killing them or feeding females drugs to stop them from reproducing.

This is just one area where humans have found themselves challenged by squirrels.

5 Squirrels and People

In general, people and squirrels get along without any problems. Squirrels have a keen intelligence. We admire the way they gather nuts and are fascinated by how they store them away for the winter.

But squirrels, especially tree squirrels, can be real nuisances. They get into bird feeders and eat birdseed. They dig up and eat flower bulbs in gardens. They gnaw their way into homes and set up house in attics and basements. They devour farm crops such as corn, wheat, oats, and barley. They eat their way through insulated utility wires and cause power outages. They strip the bark off trees, taking away the tree's protection against insects and disease. Many of

This squirrel is trying to get a meal from a bird feeder filled with food.

these trees die, hurting the logging industry that would have harvested the trees. No one has yet come up with a foolproof way to stop this behavior short of trapping and killing the squirrels.

People have been killing squirrels for a long time, but for other reasons. Early Americans hunted them for their fur and meat. Squirrel fur was once used to adorn clothing, but it is rarely used for that purpose today. Few people eat squirrel meat anymore outside of parts of the American South, where it is still considered a delicacy.

More squirrels die today from auto accidents than from hunters. As fast as squirrels are on their feet, thousands of them are run over by cars while crossing roadways. But most types of squirrels are in no danger of becoming *extinct*. There are just too many of them. There are exceptions. The red squirrel, as noted in the previous chapter, is endangered in some European countries. Another threatened species is the Delmarva fox squirrel, named for the Delmarva Peninsula that stretches from Delaware to Virginia. It was put on the U.S. Endangered Species List in 1967. Loss of habitat has been the main threat to the Delmarva fox squirrel. As forestland has been cleared for development, the Delmarva fox squirrel has had nowhere to go. It proved less adaptable than other squirrels. A recovery program to protect its remaining *habitat* was begun in 1979 and seems to be working.

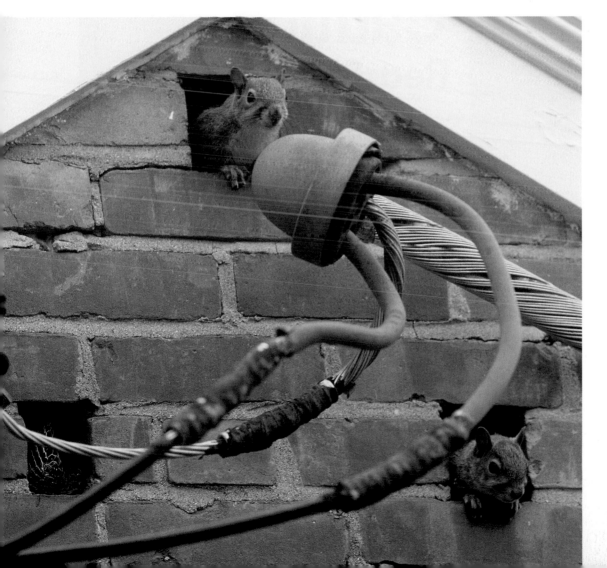

Squirrels can cause damage to wires and cables by nibbling on them.

In areas where red squirrels are endangered, signs are posted warning drivers to be extra careful and to watch for squirrels crossing the road.

Squirrels do not make good pets. They are wild animals and do not do well in captivity. But some people have, with great patience, trained squirrels to

Some squirrels in urban and suburban areas grow to trust humans and may even take food from their hands.

be pets. These pet squirrels are considered to be as intelligent as dogs. They can even be taught to perform tricks.

For most of us, however, it is simply enough to watch our squirrel neighbors scamper around our yards, chasing each other, gathering food for hard times, and climbing trees with the greatest of ease. Think of how boring our backyards would be without them!

Glossary

albino—An animal that has no pigment in the skin and fur, making the fur white and the eyes pink.

breed—To produce offspring by mating.

chambers—Rooms or compartments in the burrow of a ground squirrel or other animal that lives underground.

continent—One of the world's seven large landmasses.

dreys—Squirrel nests made out of twigs, leaves, and other plant material.

endangered—Threatened with possible extinction.

extinct—No longer in existence.

gnawing—Chewing on something with teeth.

habitat—The place where an animal lives, including the living and nonliving things in the environment.

hibernates—Goes into a deep sleep for the winter; something certain animals do to survive the cold and the scarcity of food.

immunity—A condition that makes an animal or human resistant to a disease.

litter—A group of young animals born at the same time to a female.

mammal—A warm-blooded animal that has hair or fur and nurses its young with its own milk.

molted—Shed off skin or feathers when new ones grow in.

nocturnal—Active during the night.

omnivore—An animal that eats both other animals and plants to survive.

predators—Animals that prey on, or eat, other animals to survive.

pups—Baby squirrels or the young of certain other mammals.

rodent—A kind of animal with large front teeth for gnawing.

species—Groups of living things that share the same characteristics and mate only with their own kind.

teats—Parts of a female mammal's breasts from which milk is discharged to young.

territory—An area that an animal lives in and defends from other animals of the same kind, or species.

vibrissae—The stiff whiskers on an animal's face that are sensitive to touch.

virus—An infectious agent that multiplies itself inside an animal or plant and causes disease.

Find Out More

Books

Bishop, Nic. *The Fantastic Flying Squirrel.* West Newbury, MA: Collins Educational, 2005.

Diemer, Lauren. *Squirrels* (Backyard Animals). New York: Weigl Publishing, 2008.

Murray, Peter. *Squirrels.* Chanhassen, MN: The Child's World, 2006.

Somervill, Barbara A. *Gray Squirrel* (Animal Invaders). Ann Arbor, MI: Cherry Lake Publishing, 2008.

Thorington, Richard W. Jr., and Katie E. Ferrell. *Squirrels: The Animal Answer Guide.* Baltimore, MD: Johns Hopkins University Press, 2006.

Websites

BioKids—Eastern Grey Squirrel
www.biokids.umich.edu/critters/Sciurus_
carolinensis/

Environmental Education for Kids! (EEK)—
Flying Squirrels
www.dnr.state.wi.us/Org/caer/ce/eek/critter/
mammal/flysquirrel.htm

Frequently Asked Questions about Squirrels
www.backyardnature.com/cgi-bin/gt/
tpl.h,content=501

National Geographic: Squirrel
http://animals.nationalgeographic.com/
animals/mammals/squirrel.html

Index

Page numbers for illustrations are in **boldface**.

About the Author

Steven Otfinoski is the author of numerous books about animals. He wrote five volumes in World Book's award-winning Animals of the World series. He has also written *Koalas*, *Sea Horses*, *Alligators*, *Hummingbirds*, *Dogs*, *Horses*, *Skunks*, *Storks and Cranes*, and *Pigs and Hogs* in the Animals Animals series. Otfinoski lives in Connecticut with his wife, a high school teacher and editor.